Directed Reading

Lesson: Alcohol and Your Body
TYPES OF ALCOHOLIC BEVERAGES

1. What type of process does most alcohol come from? _____________________

____

2. What is the difference between beverage alcohols and other alcohols (wood

or methanol)? ____

____

ALCOHOL IN YOUR BODY

3. Alcohol affects the central nervous system. What is the central nervous

system?

____

____

4. What happens as the amount of alcohol in your blood increases?

____

____

ALCOHOL IN THE BLOOD

________ **5.** A blood alcohol concentration, or blood alcohol level, of 0.08 percent
means that a person has 8 parts of alcohol per how many parts of blood?
    a. 100
    b. 1000
    c. 10,000
    d. 1,000,000

INDIVIDUAL REACTIONS TO ALCOHOL

6. Each person's body reacts to _____________________ a little differently.

| Directed Reading *continued*

Lesson: Immediate Effects of Alcohol
LOSING CONTROL

_______ **7.** Feeling headachy, dizzy, and nauseated after drinking is called a
   a. poor coordination.
   b. hangover.
   c. hangup.
   d. mild intoxication.

8. What is intoxication?

____

____

9. As intoxication increases, so do alcohols effects, and

_______________________ becomes impossible.

INJURY AND HARM

10. As your blood alcohol level rises, you become less likely to see risks or

predict possible harmful _______________________.

11. Alcohol can also change your _______________________ quickly, making you
happy one minute and angry the next.

Lesson: Long-Term Effects of Alcohol

12. A liver disease that affects the way in which the body processes food and gets

rid of wastes is called _______________________.

ALCOHOL'S EFFECTS

13. Alcohol can change your _______________________ , affecting your learning,
memory, and verbal skills.

14. When a person needs more of a drug to feel the original effects, it is called

_______________________.

ALCOHOL AND PREGNANCY

15. Why does drinking increase the chances that a young woman will get pregnant?

____

____

Directed Reading *continued*

16. The group of birth defects that affect an unborn baby that has been exposed

to alcohol is called _______________________.

Lesson: Alcohol and Decision-Making
ALCOHOL INFLUENCES SOCIAL DECISIONS

_______ **17.** Alcohol can relax the mental processes that restrain certain behaviors.
What are these processes called?
a. consequences
b. inhibitions
c. conversations
d. unknown elements

ALCOHOL AND VIOLENCE

_______ **18.** When a person loses control of his or her emotions, social situations
may become
a. tiring.
b. happier.
c. violent.
d. All of the above

Lesson: Alcohol, Driving, and Injuries

19. When a driver has been _______________________ bad things may happen.

A DEADLY DECISION

20. The time between when a person notices a stimulus until he or she responds

is called _______________________.

21. Why are drivers who have been drinking alcohol dangerous?

____

____

STOPPING THE INJURIES

22. The _______________________ and injuries caused by drunk driving and

accidents while operating machinery under the influence are completely

preventable.

▌Directed Reading *continued*

Lesson: Pressure to Drink
INTERNAL PRESSURES

In the blanks provided, write *I* beside internal pressures to drink and *N* beside things that *are* NOT internal pressures to drink.

_______**23.** curiosity

_______**24.** need to be accepted

_______**25.** high self-esteem

_______**26.** desire to appear adult

EXTERNAL PRESSURES

27. How do advertisements make drinking seem like a good thing to do?

____

____

28. How can seeing people drinking at parties, sporting events, or family gatherings be an external pressure to drink?

____

____

Lesson: Deciding Not to Drink
MAKING THE DECISION NOT TO DRINK

29. When you have to make an important decision like whether or not to drink

you must consider your _____________________ or, beliefs of great

importance to you.

30. You must weigh all the _____________________, or possible results, of each

of your options.

RESISTING INTERNAL PRESSURES

31. How can you deal with internal pressures that might lead you to decide to drink?

____

____

Directed Reading *continued*

Lesson: Alcoholism

32. What is alcoholism?

____

____

PHYSICAL DEPENDENCE

______**33.** The body's chemical need for a drug is called
   a. depression.
   b. physical dependence.
   c. tolerance.
   d. intoxication.

______**34.** Symptoms of alcoholism include tolerance to alcohols effects, loss of
   control, physical and emotional dependence, and
   a. carelessness.
   b. anger.
   c. a disgust toward alcohol.
   d. a strong craving to drink.

PSYCHOLOGICAL DEPENDENCE

35. Psychological dependence is a person's emotional or mental need for a

____________________________.

FACTORS THAT CONTRIBUTE TO ALCOHOLISM

36. Certain _________________________ make some people more likely to develop
alcoholism when they drink regularly.

OVERCOMING ALCOHOLISM

37. Medical care, counseling, and groups such as Alcoholics Anonymous are

important in _____________________, or learning to live without alcohol.

Concept Mapping

Lesson: Alcohol and Your Body

Use the following terms to complete the concept map below: *alcohol, small intestine, central nervous system, bloodstream, blood, stomach,* and *brain.*

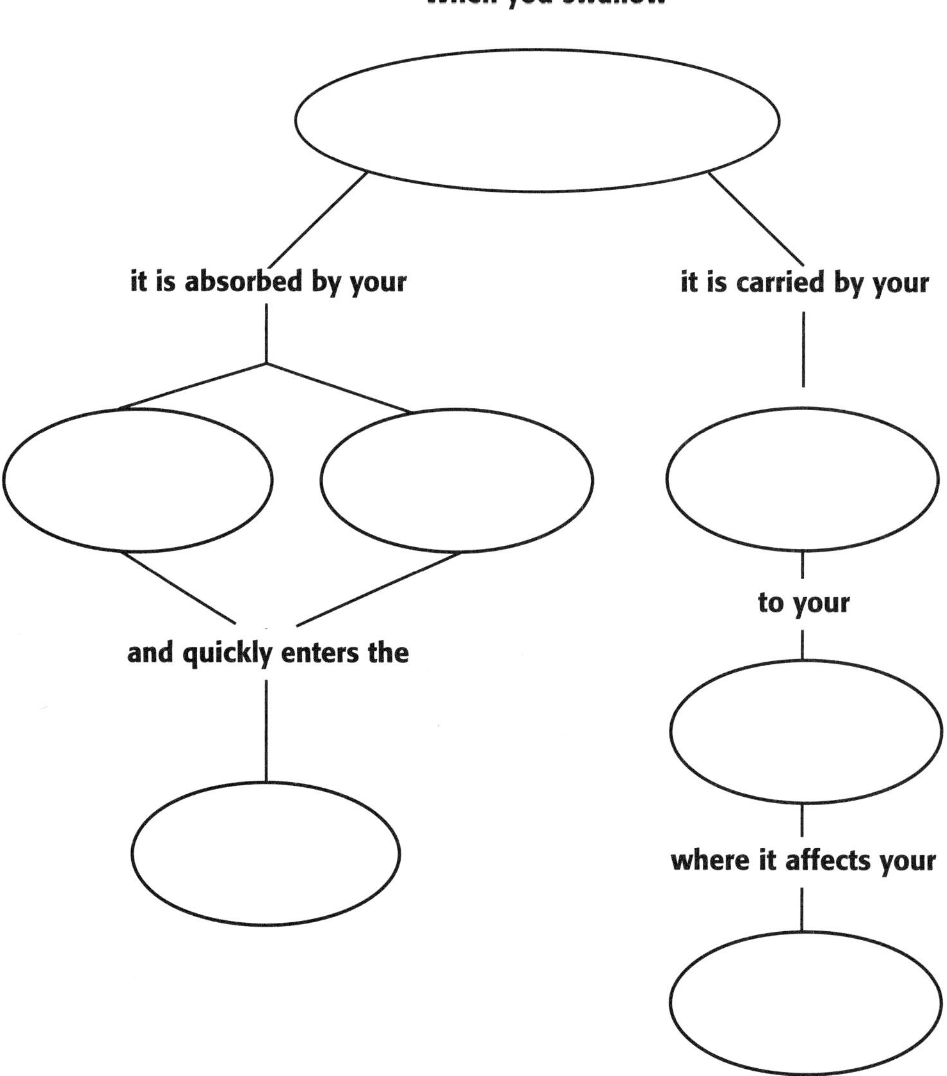

Concept Mapping

Lesson: Deciding Not to Drink

Use the following terms to create a concept map in the space below: *values, options, drink alcohol, refuse alcohol, consequences, negative affects,* **and** *feeling guilty.*

Concept Review

Lesson: Alcohol and Your Body

1. Describe what happens when alcohol enters your bloodstream.

____

____

2. What is blood alcohol concentration or blood alcohol level?

____

____

3. What are three reasons that each person's reaction to alcohol is different?

____

____

____

Lesson: Immediate Effects of Alcohol

In the blanks provided, write _A_ beside things that can be effects of alcohol and _N_ beside things that are not.

_______ **4.** decrease in self-control

_______ **5.** headache

_______ **6.** influenza

_______ **7.** poor coordination

_______ **8.** emphysema

_______ **9.** vomiting

_______**10.** hangover

_______**11.** clear thinking

12. List two risks of drinking alcohol.

____

____

| Concept Review *continued*

Lesson: Long-Term Effects of Alcohol

______**13.** A deadly disease that replaces healthy liver tissue with useless scar
tissue is called
   a. emphysema.
   b. sarcoidosis.
   c. melanoma.
   d. cirrhosis.

14. What is alcohol tolerance?

____

____

15. Why is a young woman who has been drinking at greater risk for unplanned
pregnancy?

____

____

16. What is fetal alcohol syndrome?

____

____

Lesson: Alcohol and Decision-Making

______ **17.** Alcohol lowers people's inhibitions, or restraints on doing certain
behaviors, so that they make decisions that they probably would not
have made if
   a. they hadn't been drinking.
   b. they were smarter.
   c. they weren't trying to impress people.
   d. they weren't violent people.

______ **18.** Alcohol not only lowers inhibitions, but it also causes people to lose
control of their emotions so that they may become
   a. witty.
   b. uncoordinated.
   c. violent.
   d. hard workers.

| Concept Review *continued*

Lesson: Alcohol, Driving, and Injuries

19. How does alcohol impair reaction time?

____

____

20. Groups such as SADD and MADD have worked to educate people and get stronger laws and stricter enforcement against what problem?

____

____

Lesson: Pressure to Drink

In the blanks provided, write *I* beside things that can be internal pressures to drink alcohol and and *E* beside things that are external.

_______**21.** You feel sad.

_______**22.** You see an advertisement.

_______**23.** Someone in a movie is drinking and having fun.

_______**24.** You want to numb unpleasant emotions.

_______**25.** A friend urges you to take a drink.

_______**26.** You want to act grown up.

_______**27.** You are curious about what alcohol tastes like.

_______**28.** You see an ad for alcohol that looks cold and refreshing.

Lesson: Deciding Not to Drink

_______**29.** When making an important decision like whether or not to drink, you should consider beliefs that are important to you, also called your
   a. theories.
   b. options.
   c. consequences.
   d. values.

_______**30.** After you consider your strong beliefs, you should consider the possible result of each decision, also known as
   a. consequences.
   b. theories.
   c. options.
   d. values.

Concept Review *continued*

_______**31.** The last step in making a decision is to do something, or to
   a. think.
   b. act.
   c. purchase.
   d. force.

32. Name two ways you can resist internal pressures to drink.

____

____

Lesson: Alcoholism

In the blanks provided, write *PH* beside the signs of physical dependence and *PS* beside signs of psychological dependence.

_______**33.** The body develops a tolerance for alcohol.

_______**34.** Daily routines and plans all revolve around alcohol.

_______**35.** A person has a strong craving to drink.

_______**36.** A person feels the need to drink to cope with responsibilities.

37. Identify two factors that may contribute to alcoholism.

____

____

38. What decision is the first step to recovery?

____

____

39. Name three professionals or community resources that can help people once they decide to stop drinking.

____

____

____

____

Refusal Skills

Lesson: Pressure to Drink

Describe how you would use the following refusal skills to respond to the following scenario. Remember to be clear and choose your words carefully. Describe your body language as well as your words.

You're at a big celebration. Someone you know winks at you and takes you by the arm. "This is the good punch," he or she whispers. "This punch has ZING." You're pretty sure that means someone added alcohol to the punch. "Let me get you some," says the person who is holding your arm.

1. **Say no.** How do you tell the person holding your arm that you don't want any of the punch with "zing"?

____

____

2. **Offer an alternative.** What other drinks could you suggest?

____

____

3. **Stand your ground.** What would you do if your friend keeps telling you how great the punch is and urging you to try some?

____

____

4. **Walk away.** Describe how you would get out of the situation.

____

____

5. **Plan ahead.** What could you do to avoid this situation? Who can help you practice refusing this action?

____

____

6. **Have a support system.** Who will stand by you when you make this decision? How can you use these people as support when refusing to do this action?

____

____

Refusal Skills

Lesson: Pressure to Drink

Design a board game to remind yourself and others of refusal skills. Remember to be clear and choose your words carefully.

Board games are good ways to have fun and practice refusal skills at the same time. In the space below, sketch a design of a board game with at least 10 squares, some way to move around the board, and opportunities to make decisions about alcohol and to practice avoiding and refusing alcohol.

Name _________________________________ Class _______________ Date _____________

Decision-Making Skills

Lesson: Alcohol and Decision-Making

Read the following situation. Then, follow the steps below to decide what you would do in this situation.

You are going to spend a week at your grandparents' house. The last time you were there, a cousin and his friends were drinking beer and jokingly offered you some. You feel you should make some decisions before you get there about what to do if they offer you some beer this time.

1. Identify the problem. What decision do you have to make?

____

____

2. Consider your values. What is important to you?

____

____

3. List the options. What possible actions could you take?

____

____

____

4. Weigh the consequences. List the pros and cons of each option.

____

____

____

5. Decide and act. Describe what you will do. Explain your decision.

____

____

6. Evaluate your choice. How do you feel about the action you took? Did you make a good decision? Would you take a different action if faced with the same scenario again?

____

____

____

Decision-Making Skills

Lesson: Deciding Not to Drink

In the space below, design a booklet to remind yourself of ways to make good decisions about alcohol.

Design and make a pocket-sized booklet that can remind you of ways to make good decisions. Include the decision-making steps, some refusal skills, and some inspirational quotes and notes to yourself. Keep the booklet where you can review it often.

Cross-Disciplinary: Science

Lesson: Alcohol and Your Body

Review the information in your textbook on how the body processes alcohol. Then, find information on how your body processes healthful foods and beverages. Make a chart in the space below to compare how the two processes are similar and how they are different.

Cross-Disciplinary: Language Arts

Lesson: Alcoholism

Choose one of the two projects described below to complete.

1. Write a letter to someone, real or imagined, who is struggling with alcoholism. Be as specific and detailed as you can. Tell the person how you feel about him or her, what qualities of his or her personality you admire and how you feel about how alcoholism affects his or her life and yours. Encourage the individual to begin the process of recovery. Use the space below to organize your ideas.

____

____

____

____

____

____

____

2. Write a poem that has something to do with alcoholism. It could be from your point of view, telling how good life can be without alcohol. It could be from the point of view of a person with alcoholism telling about his or her struggle. You may choose any poetry form, but be consistent throughout, and give specific, realistic details and images. Use the space below to organize your ideas.

____

____

____

____

____

____

____

Assessment

Quiz

Lesson: Alcohol and Your Body

Write the letter of the correct answer in the space provided.

______ **1.** What part of the body does alcohol mainly affect?
   a. digestive system
   b. respiratory system
   c. central nervous system
   d. circulatory system

______ **2.** Why does the amount of alcohol concentrated in your blood increase so rapidly if you drink more than one drink an hour?
   a. Your blood slows down.
   b. The liver has shut down.
   c. Your liver can't process it fast enough.
   d. You don't have enough food in your stomach.

______ **3.** How a person reacts to alcohol is affected by his or her health, sex, the amount of sleep he or she has gotten, and
   a. his or her skin tone.
   b. the time of day.
   c. the type of drinking container used.
   d. any medications the person is taking.

Match the definitions with the correct term. Write the letter in the space provided.

______ **4.** the percentage of alcohol in the blood

______ **5.** the brain and spinal cord

______ **6.** drug that slows body functioning

a. central nervous system

b. depressant

c. BAC

Quiz

Lesson: Immediate Effects of Alcohol

Write the letter of the correct answer in the space provided.

______ **1.** As you drink you become mildly intoxicated and may feel lightheaded; as intoxication increases it becomes difficult to
  a. drink more.
  b. feel emotions.
  c. get violent.
  d. do anything requiring coordination.

______ **2.** What are some of the risks you take if you decide to drink one evening?
  a. mood swings and loss of coordination
  b. loss of skin and hair tissue
  c. cancer and tumors
  d. respiratory diseases

______ **3.** If you drink way too much alcohol at one time what do you risk?
  a. being silly
  b. having people laugh at you
  c. poisoning and death
  d. walking crooked

Match the definitions with the correct term. Write the letter in the space provided.

______ **4.** a type of drug overdose

______ **5.** the changes produced by drinking

______ **6.** uncomfortable physical effects from alcohol

a. intoxication

b. alcohol poisoning

c. hangover

Quiz

Lesson: Long-Term Effects of Alcohol

Write the letter of the correct answer in the space provided.

______ **1.** Drinking before your brain is fully mature may cause what to happen?
    a. Your brain becomes impaired.
    b. You lose your hair.
    c. You get cancer.
    d. Your skin becomes wrinkled.

______ **2.** What part of your body does alcohol-related cirrhosis affect?
    a. brain
    b. central nervous system
    c. liver
    d. blood

______ **3.** Why are pregnant women warned not to drink alcohol?
    a. It can cause weight gain.
    b. It can lead to divorce.
    c. It can cause fetal alcohol syndrome.
    d. It can lead to extra-long pregnancies.

Match the definitions with the correct term. Write the letter in the space provided.

______ **4.** more alcohol needed for same effect   **a.** cirrhosis

______ **5.** group of birth defects caused by alcohol   **b.** tolerance

______ **6.** disease that turns liver to scar tissue   **c.** fetal alcohol syndrome

Quiz

Lesson: Alcohol and Decision-Making

Write the letter of the correct answer in the space provided.

_______ **1.** What is a word for the mental or psychological processes that restrain
your actions, emotions, and thoughts?
   a. restrainers
   b. inhibitions
   c. demotions
   d. consequences

_______ **2.** When you've drunk some alcohol it's harder to
   a. act funny.
   b. party.
   c. be with people.
   d. recognize risks.

_______ **3.** Fights, crimes, abuse, vandalism, and robbery are more likely if what
is involved?
   a. cars
   b. property
   c. alcohol
   d. depression

Match the definitions with the correct term. Write the letter in the space provided.

_______ **4.** restraint of actions and emotions

_______ **5.** one of the effects of alcohol

_______ **6.** what happens as a result of an action

a. unclear thinking

b. inhibitions

c. consequences

Quiz

Lesson: Alcohol, Driving, and Injuries

Write the letter of the correct answer in the space provided.

_______ **1.** When a person drinks one drink, his or her ability to drive an automobile is
 a. unchanged.
 b. better than ever.
 c. terrible.
 d. somewhat affected.

_______ **2.** The only sure way to avoid alcohol-related injuries and death is to ride with someone only if
 a. he or she can walk straight.
 b. you are in the front seat.
 c. he or she has not been drinking.
 d. he or she has had less than three drinks.

_______ **3.** Groups like SADD and MADD and a combination of stronger laws and stricter enforcement have reduced
 a. the number of people who drink.
 b. the amount of alcohol sold.
 c. the number of alcohol-related car accidents.
 d. the number of alcohol-related suicides.

Match the definitions with the correct term. Write the letter in the space provided.

_______ **4.** one of the skills reduced by alcohol

_______ **5.** a sight, sound, or thought causing reaction

_______ **6.** the time between a stimulus and reaction

a. stimulus

b. reaction time

c. concentration

Quiz

Lesson: Pressure to Drink

Write the letter of the correct answer in the space provided.

_______ **1.** Most teens have an inner need to be part of a
   a. team.
   b. group.
   c. school.
   d. class.

_______ **2.** Low self-esteem, trying to escape unpleasant feelings, and wanting to impress others are all reasons teens may
   a. drink.
   b. drive.
   c. be careful.
   d. give up.

_______ **3.** Seeing people drinking at parties, sporting events, and restaurants can make you think that
   a. everyone drinks.
   b. everyone drinks too much.
   c. everyone is grown up.
   d. everyone is looking at you.

Match the definitions with the correct term. Write the letter in the space provided.

_______ **4.** pressures from outside yourself

_______ **5.** pressures from inside yourself

_______ **6.** promotions designed to get you to buy
   a product

a. internal

b. advertisements

c. external

Quiz

Lesson: Deciding Not to Drink

Write the letter of the correct answer in the space provided.

_______ **1.** When you are trying to make a big decision you should
  a. follow someone's example.
  b. think about what your values are.
  c. drink some alcohol to help you think.
  d. respond to the pressures you feel.

_______ **2.** If you're feeling lonely or bad about yourself you should
  a. shake it off.
  b. hang out with friends.
  c. get some new friends.
  d. talk to an adult you trust.

_______ **3.** When you're feeling a lot of pressure you should
  a. find something to do.
  b. take something to relax you.
  c. take some time to think.
  d. go have a good time.

Match the descriptions with the correct term. Write the letter in the space provided.

_______ **4.** feelings and needs inside you

_______ **5.** beliefs that are important to you

_______ **6.** possible results of your actions

a. values

b. consequences

c. internal pressure

Quiz

Lesson: Alcoholism

Write the letter of the correct answer in the space provided.

_______ **1.** Physical dependence has to do with the body, while psychological dependence has to do with the
   a. people around you.
   b. values and beliefs that you have.
   c. need for a psychiatrist.
   d. emotions and thoughts.

_______ **2.** When a person's friendships, work, daily routine, and the way he or she spends money all revolve around alcohol, it is likely the person
   a. has alcoholism.
   b. can easily stop drinking.
   c. is already too damaged to quit.
   d. has self esteem.

_______ **3.** The first step to overcoming alcoholism is deciding to
   a. drink less.
   b. only drink at night.
   c. stop drinking.
   d. quit work.

Match the descriptions with the correct term. Write the letter in the space provided.

_______ **4.** physical, emotional, or mental need

_______ **5.** learning to live without alcohol

_______ **6.** dependence on alcohol

a. recovery

b. alcoholism

c. dependence

Chapter Test

Alcohol
USING VOCABULARY

Use the terms from the following list to complete each sentence below. A term may be used only once. Some terms will not be used.

psychological   blood alcohol concentration   relapse   dependence
recovery   tolerance   inhibition   physical

1. Whenever Sam has had a rough day, he unwinds with a couple of beers. It's hard for him now to feel relaxed without them because he has developed

   a _________________ dependence on alcohol.

2. When a policeman stops someone he thinks might have been drinking, one

   test he can use is the _________________ test to see how much alcohol is in the person's blood.

3. Some people drink alcohol to relax, but after a while they find that they require more alcohol to relax because they have built up a

   _________________ .

4. Maria's uncle goes to Alcoholics Anonymous at least once a week as part of

   his _________________ from alcohol.

UNDERSTANDING CONCEPTS

Write the letter of the correct answer in the space provided.

_______ 5. What effect does alcohol have on a person's ability to make decisions?
   a. makes it easier to think
   b. calms the emotions
   c. increases inhibitions
   d. makes it hard to see risks

_______ 6. When alcohol gets to the brain, it impairs judgment, coordination, and
   a. lung capacity.
   b. vision.
   c. nerve development.
   d. All of the above

_______ 7. Which of the following is an internal pressure that might make some-one more likely to try alcohol?
   a. cirrhosis
   b. low self-esteem
   c. refusal skills
   d. confidence

_______ 8. The brain and spinal cord are part of what system?
   a. circulatory
   b. digestive
   c. nervous
   d. brain

| Chapter Test *continued*

_________ **9.** What is the only thing that can get your BAC down?
    a. coffee   **c.** food
    b. a shower   **d.** time

_________ **10.** Alcohol poisoning
    a. is a drug overdose.
    b. is caused by drinking too much alcohol.
    c. can be fatal.
    d. All of the above

_________ **11.** Alcohol reaches the brain
    a. through the small intestine.
    b. in 10–15 heartbeats.
    c. through the heart.
    d. All of the above

_________ **12.** The best way to avoid injuries and death from drunk driving is to
    a. wear your seat belt.
    b. never ride with someone who has been drinking.
    c. take public transportation.
    d. None of the above

_________ **13.** The body's chemical need for a drug is called
    a. tolerance.
    b. physical dependence.
    c. alcoholism.
    d. None of the above

_________ **14.** Which of the following is a factor that might influence whether a person develops alcoholism?
    a. height   **c.** knowledge about alcohol
    b. reaction time   **d.** genes

15. What is a depressant?

____

____

16. What is intoxication?

____

____

17. What is fetal alcohol syndrome?

____

____

❙ Chapter Test *continued*

CRITICAL THINKING

18. Explain what a hangover is and how someone gets a hangover.

____

____

____

____

____

19. Why is a person more likely to be injured while he or she is drinking?

____

____

____

____

____

20. Why does refusing to drink alcohol decrease your risk of getting injured or engaging in unhealthy behaviors?

____

____

____

____

____

____

Chapter Test *continued*

CONCEPT MAPPING

21. Use the following terms to create a concept map in the space below: *alcohol, alcoholism, recovery, dependence, physical, psychological,* and *cirrhosis.*

Performance-Based Assessment

How Alcohol Affects You

INTRODUCTION

You've read about how alcohol affects the body, mind, and emotions. This exercise will allow you to show the things you have learned.

OBJECTIVE

- Keep in mind that your teacher will be observing and grading your in-class behavior as well as your written responses. In particular, your teacher will be noting your ability to follow the given procedures, how well you follow classroom safety guidelines, and your methods and reasoning in solving problems.
- Try not to let what others are doing influence your work. Remember that a problem often has several acceptable solutions.
- Do not talk to other students unless you are working in a group. Talk only to members of your group and try not to disturb other students.
- Use only the materials provided.

MATERIALS AND EQUIPMENT

- cards with situations on them
- box

PROCEDURE

1. Form groups of two or three. Each group will draw a situation out of a box and create a skit that dramatizes a reaction to that situation. The skit should demonstrate understanding of the material learned in this chapter. Each member of the group should participate in some way.

2. Each person will take notes on the other students' performance, writing each individual's name, what you liked about his or her response, and one thing you would have done differently. Turn these notes in to your teacher.

ANALYSIS

At the end of class respond to this question.

3. Do you feel this exercise demonstrated fairly your knowledge about alcohol? Why or why not?

____

____

____

____

Datasheet for In-Text Activity

Alcohol and Your Body

1. With a partner, create a list of alcohols effects on body systems and a list of alcohols effects on emotions.

Effects on Body Systems

Effects on Emotions

____

____

____

____

____

____

____

____

____

____

____

____

____

____

ANALYSIS

2. Compare the two lists, and note any similarities or differences.

____

____

____

____

____

3. Based on the information you have collected, design and make a poster or pamphlet warning people about alcohol consumption.

Activity

Life Skills: Evaluating Media Messages

Lesson: Immediate Effects of Alcohol

Find five newspaper or magazine articles or advertisements involving alcohol. For each article or advertisement, give a brief summary and explain what you think you learned about alcohol and society's opinion of it.

1. Summary ____

____

What I learned ____

____

2. Summary ____

____

What I learned ____

____

3. Summary ____

____

What I learned ____

____

4. Summary ____

____

What I learned ____

____

5. Summary ____

____

What I learned ____

____

Activity

Life Skills: Coping

Lesson: Long-Term Effects of Alcohol

Think about what it would be like to have either a chronic illness, such as cirrhosis of the liver, caused by alcohol abuse, or problems (birth defects) caused by fetal alcohol syndrome. Then, answer the three questions below. In your descriptions, consider what you've seen or know about someone who may actually have one of these conditions.

1. How would a person's life be affected by the condition or illness? Describe what his or her limitations, challenges, or special needs might be. How would a person manage daily activities with this condition?

____

____

____

____

2. How might the people around this person be affected by the disease or condition? How must they help the person?

____

____

____

____

3. What could you do to help a person who has a chronic illness or limitations due to birth defects?

____

____

____

____

____

Activity

Enrichment Activity

Lesson: Alcohol and Your Body

Alcohol has been a part of most societies in the world for a long time. Find a historical or literary incident involving alcohol. For example, at the Battle of Trenton, New Jersey, General Washington's men surprised the Hessians (who were fighting for the British) the day after Christmas when the Hessians were still recovering from having celebrated with alcohol.

When you have found your incident, write a brief summary of the incident, including the effect you think the alcohol had on the incident. What would have been different if alcohol had not been involved? Use this space below to take notes.

____

____

____

____

Lesson: Immediate Effects of Alcohol

Although alcohol can impair judgment, vision, and coordination, people are still considered responsible for what they do when they are intoxicated. Is this fair? How can a person be responsible when a drug has affected his or her mind? Would it be more fair if people were not responsible for their behavior when they have been drinking? Why or why not?

Write a paragraph or brief essay expressing your opinion on these questions. Use the space below to organize your ideas.

____

____

____

____

____

____

Lesson: Long-Term Effects of Alcohol

Are long-term effects of alcohol as well known as long-term effects of behaviors like smoking? Brainstorm some catchy phrases that will keep
people's attention focused on the problem of these long-term effects of alcohol.

Set a timer for 3 minutes. In that time brainstorm as many phrases as you can. Write them all down in the space below, no matter how ridiculous they seem. At the end of 3 minutes, choose the three phrases you think are the best. Then, pick one phrase, and use it to create a 30-second radio commercial.

____

____

____

____

____

____

Lesson: Alcohol and Decision-Making

Write a paragraph about whether you think one the opinion paragraphs below is true—or whether the truth is somewhere in between. What, in your opinion, is the right way to approach this topic?

Opinion 1: Hearing information about the problems with alcohol or another drug sometimes creates denial in students. They may think, "Alcohol isn't so bad. I know people who drink alcohol all the time, and none of this bad stuff ever happens to them."

Opinion 2: If students are presented information that suggests that alcohol may be all right under some circumstances, they will feel that it's fine to drink as much as they want. Even hearing a recovering person with alcoholism may make them think that they can try alcohol and then recover and go on to have a wonderful life.

Lesson: Alcohol, Driving, and Injuries

Figure out a way to simulate slowed reaction time. Design the simulation so that students would be asked to perform a simple, everyday task with their reaction time slowed in some way so they could begin to understand how slowed reaction time can affect a person's performance. Use only materials that are commonly found at home or at school. Avoid any activity where someone could get hurt or embarrassed in any way. Before you actually carry out the simulation, show your plan to your teacher for approval. Use the space below to brainstorm ideas.

Lesson: Pressure to Drink

Look for biographical sketches or biographies of people you admire. Choose one person who had many inner and external pressures to make bad choices, but who managed to stay healthy and have a successful life. Write a brief biography about the person, listing his or her name, birth date, place of birth, and a summary of the person's life experiences.

Lesson: Deciding Not to Drink

Think hard about the things that may make teens feel sad, inadequate, or lonely.
Write a list of pressures teens face and suggestions on how to deal with them,
other than turning to alcohol for "comfort."

____

____

____

____

____

____

____

____

____

____

____

____

____

Lesson: Alcoholism

Draw a picture, sketch, or diagram that demonstrates the differences between the
way that a casual drinker reacts to alcohol and the way that a person with alcoholism reacts to alcohol. Show physical differences and indicate emotional and
mental differences.

Name _________________________________ Class _______________ Date _____________

Health Inventory

Alcohol

Use the following questions to help you evaluate the risk factors that influence your choices about using alcohol.

yes	no		points
❑	❑	**1.** Have you made a firm decision to avoid alcohol at least until you are of legal age?	30 points
❑	❑	**2.** Have you practiced refusal skills?	30 points
❑	❑	**3.** Do you avoid situations where you might be at risk because of someone else's drinking?	10 points
❑	❑	**4.** Do you "talk back" to advertisements about alcohol by thinking about the true risks of alcohol use?	8 points
❑	❑	**5.** Do you feel good about your ability to make decisions for yourself?	5 points
❑	❑	**6.** Do the people you most admire drink a lot?	5 points
❑	❑	**7.** Do you think about the benefits of staying alcohol free?	8 points
❑	❑	**8.** Do you feel good about your ability to say no and stick to it even if people pressure you?	5 points
❑	❑	**9.** Do you save any risk-taking urges you have for healthy outlets such as sports?	5 points
❑	❑	**10.** Do you have close friends who are committed to an alcohol-free lifestyle?	10 points

Add up the points for all of the questions to which you answered yes.

Look at the scale to see how much of a problem alcohol poses to your health.

SCALE	
90–116	You have a strong commitment to staying alcohol free, and you have the personal skills to help you keep your commitment.
60–90	Thinking through your values and goals for your life and making a firm decision about alcohol use will help you make good decisions.
40–60	You have some risk of being vulnerable to pressures to use alcohol.
20–40	You would benefit from learning more about the risks of alcohol use and strengthening your refusal skills.
Less than 20	You need to increase your understanding of what alcohol is and what dangers it poses for you.

Activity

Health Behavior Contract

Alcohol

My Goals: I, _________________________________, will accomplish one or more of the following goals:

I will not drink alcoholic beverages.

I will avoid places where I may be pressured to drink alcoholic beverages.

I will use refusal skills if I am offered alcoholic beverages.

Other: ____

____

My Reasons: By refusing to drink alcoholic beverages, I will be less likely to do things that could lead to injury, violence, disease, or death. I will also maintain my overall physical, social, mental, and emotional health.

Other: ____

____

My Values: Personal values that will help me meet my goals are

____

____

My Plan: The actions I will take to meet my goals are

____

____

____

____

Evaluation: I will use my Health Journal to keep a log of actions I took to fulfill this contract. After 1 month, I will evaluate my goals. I will adjust my plan if my goals are not being met. If my goals are being met, I will consider setting additional goals.

Signed _________________________________

Date _________________________________

Name _________________________________ Class ______________ Date ______________

At-Home Activity

Dreams and Hopes for the Future

Student: Write a letter to your parents or guardians. In the first paragraph, tell them your hopes and dreams for the future. In the next paragraphs, tell them how choosing to drink alcohol might affect those hopes and dreams. Deliver the letter and discuss it with them.

____

____

____

____

____

____

____

____

____

____

____

____

____

The signatures below verify that our discussion has take place.

____ ________________

Student Signature   Class Period

____ ________________

Parent or Guardian Signature   Date

Activity
Actividad En Casa

Los sueños y las esperanzas para el futuro

Estudiante: Escríbale(s) una carta a su(s) padres/tutor. En los primeros párrafos, dígale(s) sus sueños y esperanzas para el futuro. En los párrafos siguientes, hable de los efectos posibles sobre su futuro ideal si Ud. optara por tomar el alcohol. Entréguele(s) su carta y discútala con él/ella/ellos.

____

____

____

____

____

____

____

____

____

____

____

____

____

____

Las firmas verifican que discutimos esta actividad juntos.

_______________________________   _______________________________

Firma de Estudiante   Período de Clase(la Salud)

_______________________________   _______________________________

Firma de Padre/Madre/Tutor   Fecha

Lesson Plan

Lesson: Alcohol and Your Body

Pacing

45 minutes

Objectives

1. Describe how the body processes alcohol.

2. Explain blood alcohol concentration.

3. Identify three factors that affect an individual's reaction to alcohol.

Standards Covered

1.3 Explain the impact of personal health behaviors on the functioning of body systems.

KEY

SE = Student Edition   **ATE** = Annotated Teacher Edition
CRF = Chapter Resource File

CHAPTER OPENER

❏ **Health IQ, SE** To assess student knowledge about Alcohol, have students answer the Health IQ questions. Answers are at the bottom of the test.

FOCUS

❏ **Bellringer, ATE** Students list as many alcohol products as they can.

❏ **Bellringer Transparency** Use this transparency as students enter the classroom and find their seats.

❏ **Start Off Write, SE** Ask students to write an answer to the following question: "What happens to your body when you drink alcohol?"

MOTIVATE

❏ **Discussion, Alcohol and People, ATE** Explore students perceptions of alcohol and alcohol use. [GENERAL]

TEACH

❏ **Teaching Transparency, Alcohol's Path Through Your Body** Use this transparency as you do the Using the Figure activity.

❏ **Using the Figure, Alcohol in the Body, SE** Students draw alcohol's path through the body as it is described in the SE. [BASIC]

Lesson Plan *continued*

❑ **Hands-On Activity, Alcohol and Your Body, SE** This activity compares alcohol's effects on the body and the emotions.

❑ **Datasheets for In-Text Activity, Alcohol and Your Body, CRF** Students use this worksheet to answer the questions from the Hands-On Activity. [GENERAL]

CLOSE

❑ **Lesson Quiz, ATE** Students answer 2 questions about alcohol.

❑ **Lesson Quiz, CRF** Students answer 6 questions about alcohol.

❑ **Concept Review, CRF** This exercise reinforces the material covered in the lesson.

HOMEWORK

❑ **Lesson Review, SE** Assign questions 1–5 for review, homework, or quiz.

❑ **At-Home Activity, CRF** This activity requires students to discuss their hopes and dreams, and the effects of alcohol use on those dreams.

❑ **Concept Mapping, CRF** Students create a concept map related to alcohol's path through the body. [GENERAL]

OTHER RESOURCE OPTIONS

❑ **Internet Connect** Blood Alcohol Concentration, HealthLinks Code HD4016. Students research Internet sources about blood alcohol levels.

❑ **go.hrw.com** For worksheets, videos, and other teaching aids related to this chapter, visit the HRW Web site and type in the keyword HD4AL8.

❑ **VideoSelect** Videos related to the chapter topics may be found at go.hrw.com. Type in the keyword HD4AL8V.

❑ **Guided Audio CD Program Alcohol** The audio program is a reading of the chapter content for ELL students, auditory learners, and struggling readers.

❑ **Directed Reading, CRF** This worksheet is to be filled out as students read the chapter. [BASIC]

❑ **Enrichment Activity, CRF** Students will examine alcohol use throughout history and in other cultures. [ADVANCED]

❑ **Cross-Disciplinary: Science, CRF** Students compare digestion of healthful foods and beverages with the body's processing of alcohol. [GENERAL]

Lesson Plan

Lesson: Immediate Effects of Alcohol

Pacing

20 minutes

Objectives

1. Describe how alcohol affects a person's behavior.

2. Identify two risks of drinking alcohol.

Standards Covered

1.1 Explain the relationship between positive health behaviors and the prevention of injury, illness, disease, and other health problems.

> **KEY**
> **SE** = Student Edition   **ATE** = Annotated Teacher Edition
> **CRF** = Chapter Resource File

FOCUS

❑ **Bellringer, ATE** Students describe how a person acts when he or she drinks alcohol.

❑ **Bellringer Transparency** Use this transparency as students enter the classroom and find their seats.

❑ **Start Off Write, SE** Ask students to write an answer to the following question: "What are some effects of drinking alcohol?"

MOTIVATE

❑ **Activity, Skit, ATE** Organize the class into groups and have each group perform its skit for the class. Afterward discuss what the skits had in common. **[GENERAL]**

TEACH

❑ **Group Activity, Comic Book, ATE** Student groups create comic books illustrating the short-term effects of alcohol. **[GENERAL]**

❑ **Life Skills: Evaluating Media Messages, CRF** Students analyze articles and advertisements about alcohol. **[GENERAL]**

CLOSE

❑ **Lesson Quiz, ATE** Students answer 3 questions about alcohol's effects.

❑ **Lesson Quiz, CRF** Students answer 6 questions about alcohol's effects.

❑ **Concept Review, CRF** This exercise reinforces the material covered in the lesson.

Lesson Plan *continued*

HOMEWORK

❏ **Lesson Review, SE** Assign questions 1–5 for review, homework, or quiz.

❏ **Directed Reading, CRF** This worksheet is to be filled out as students read the chapter. **[Basic]**

OTHER RESOURCE OPTIONS

❏ **go.hrw.com** For worksheets, videos, and other teaching aids related to this chapter, visit the HRW Web site and type in the keyword HD4AL8.

❏ **VideoSelect** Videos related to the chapter topics may be found at go.hrw.com. Type in the keyword HD4AL8V.

❏ **Guided Audio CD Program Alcohol** The audio program is a reading of the chapter content for ELL students, auditory learners, and struggling readers.

❏ **Enrichment Activity, CRF** Students express their opinion on whether someone should be held responsible for actions performed "under the influence" of alcohol. **[ADVANCED]**

Lesson Plan

Lesson: Long-Term Effects of Alcohol

Pacing

25 minutes

Objectives

1. Identify two long-term effects of drinking alcohol.

2. Explain why it is dangerous for pregnant women to drink alcohol.

Standards Covered

1.1 Explain the relationship between positive health behaviors and the prevention of injury, illness, disease, and other health problems.

KEY

SE = Student Edition　　**ATE** = Annotated Teacher Edition
CRF = Chapter Resource File

FOCUS

❑ **Bellringer, ATE**　Students explain why drinking alcohol may be especially harmful to teens.

❑ **Bellringer Transparency**　Use this transparency as students enter the classroom and find their seats.

❑ **Start Off Write, SE**　Ask students to write an answer to the following question: "Why is it dangerous for a pregnant woman to drink alcohol?"

MOTIVATE

❑ **Group Activity, Alcohol and Body Systems, ATE**　Four student groups research and present findings on how alcohol affects the following body systems: circulatory, nervous, respiratory, and muscular. **[GENERAL]**

TEACH

❑ **Debate, Drinking During Pregnancy, ATE**　Students debate whether women who drink alcohol during pregnancy should be prosecuted for child abuse. **[GENERAL]**

❑ **Concept Mapping, ATE**　Students complete a concept map on various diseases that can be alcohol related.

Lesson Plan *continued*

CLOSE

- ❏ **Lesson Quiz, ATE** Students answer 2 questions about the long-term effects of alcohol.
- ❏ **Lesson Quiz, CRF** Students answer 6 questions about long-term effects of alcohol.
- ❏ **Concept Review, CRF** This exercise reinforces the material covered in the lesson.

HOMEWORK

- ❏ **Lesson Review, SE** Assign questions 1–5 for review, homework, or quiz.
- ❏ **Life Skills: Coping, CRF** Students complete a worksheet on coping with birth defects and chronic illnesses.

OTHER RESOURCE OPTIONS

- ❏ **Internet Connect** Drug and Alcohol Abuse, HealthLinks Code HD4029. Students research Internet sources about alcohol abuse.
- ❏ **go.hrw.com** For worksheets, videos, and other teaching aids related to this chapter, visit the HRW Web site and type in the keyword HD4AL8.
- ❏ **VideoSelect** Videos related to the chapter topics may be found at go.hrw.com. Type in the keyword HD4AL8V.
- ❏ **Guided Audio CD Program Alcohol** The audio program is a reading of the chapter content for ELL students, auditory learners, and struggling readers.
- ❏ **Directed Reading, CRF** This worksheet is to be filled out as students read the chapter. [BASIC]
- ❏ **Enrichment Activity, CRF** Students make slogans to advertise the long-term effects of alcohol. [ADVANCED]

Lesson Plan

Lesson: Alcohol and Decision-Making

Pacing

25 minutes

Objectives

1. Explain how drinking alcohol affects a person's ability to make decisions.

2. Describe the relationship between alcohol and violence.

Standards Covered

1.1 Explain the relationship between positive health behaviors and the prevention of injury, illness, disease, and premature death.

1.4 Analyze how family, peers, and community influence the health of individuals.

4.2 Analyze how messages from media and other sources influence health behaviors.

4.4 Analyze how information from peers influences health.

6.2 Analyze how health-related decisions are influenced by individuals, family and community values.

6.3 Predict how decisions regarding health behaviors have consequences for self and others.

KEY
SE = Student Edition   **ATE** = Annotated Teacher Edition
CRF = Chapter Resource File

FOCUS

❑ **Bellringer, ATE** Students list inhibitions that people lose when under the influence of alcohol and possible effects of losing each inhibition.

❑ **Bellringer Transparency** Use this transparency as students enter the classroom and find their seats.

❑ **Start Off Write, SE** Ask students to write an answer to the following question: "How does alcohol affect a person's ability to make decisions?"

MOTIVATE

❑ **Activity, Role-Playing, ATE** Students understand through role-playing how alcohol consumption can have negative consequences.

Lesson Plan *continued*

TEACH

❏ **Discussion, Stories of Alcohol Abuse, ATE** Students discuss the role alcohol played in violent incidents and whether they think such stories are rare or common. [BASIC]

❏ **Decision-Making Skills, CRF** Students complete the worksheet by deciding how to prepare for a cousin's offer of beer. [GENERAL]

CLOSE

❏ **Lesson Quiz, ATE** Students answer 2 questions about alcohol and decision making.

❏ **Lesson Quiz, CRF** Students answer 6 questions about alcohol and decision making.

❏ **Concept Review, CRF** This exercise reinforces the material covered in the lesson.

HOMEWORK

❏ **Lesson Review, SE** Assign questions 1–4 for review, homework, or quiz.

❏ **Directed Reading, CRF** This worksheet is to be filled out as students read the chapter. [BASIC]

OTHER RESOURCE OPTIONS

❏ **go.hrw.com** For worksheets, videos, and other teaching aids related to this chapter, visit the HRW Web site and type in the keyword HD4AL8.

❏ **VideoSelect** Videos related to the chapter topics may be found at go.hrw.com. Type in the keyword HD4AL8V.

❏ **Guided Audio CD Program Alcohol** The audio program is a reading of the chapter content for ELL students, auditory learners, and struggling readers.

❏ **Enrichment Activity, CRF** Students debate how information on the dangers of alcohol and other drugs should be presented. [ADVANCED]

Lesson Plan

Lesson: Alcohol, Driving, and Injuries

Pacing

20 minutes

Objectives

1. Explain how alcohol impairs a person's ability to drive.

2. Identify three types of injuries, other than driving injuries, in which alcohol may be involved.

Standards Covered

1.1 Explain the relationship between positive health behaviors and the prevention of injury, illness, disease and other health problems.

1.4 Analyze how family, peers, and community influence the health of individuals.

3.4 Develop strategies to improve or maintain person, family and community health.

4.2 Analyze how messages from media and other sources influence health behaviors.

6.3 Predict how decisions regarding health behaviors have consequences for self and others.

KEY

SE = Student Edition **ATE** = Annotated Teacher Edition
CRF = Chapter Resource File

FOCUS

❑ **Bellringer, ATE** Students list the possible consequences for a teenager who was driving after drinking alcohol.

❑ **Bellringer Transparency** Use this transparency as students enter the classroom and find their seats.

❑ **Start Off Write, SE** Ask students to write an answer to the following question: "Why is drinking and driving so dangerous?"

MOTIVATE

❑ **Activity, Drunk Drivers, ATE** Students design posters that warn young people about drunk driving or about accepting a ride with someone who is drunk. [GENERAL]

TEACH

❏ **Demonstration, 1 Driver in 10, ATE** Use index cards to illustrate statistics about drunk driving. [GENERAL]

CLOSE

❏ **Lesson Quiz, ATE** Students answer a three-part question about alcohol, driving, and injuries.

❏ **Lesson Quiz, CRF** Students answer 6 questions about alcohol, driving, and injuries.

❏ **Concept Review, CRF** This exercise reinforces the material covered in the lesson.

HOMEWORK

❏ **Lesson Review, SE** Assign questions 1–5 for review, homework, or quiz.

OTHER RESOURCE OPTIONS

❏ **go.hrw.com** For worksheets, videos, and other teaching aids related to this chapter, visit the HRW Web site and type in the keyword HD4AL8.

❏ **VideoSelect** Videos related to the chapter topics may be found at go.hrw.com. Type in the keyword HD4AL8V.

❏ **Guided Audio CD Program Alcohol** The audio program is a reading of the chapter content for ELL students, auditory learners, and struggling readers.

❏ **Directed Reading, CRF** This worksheet is to be filled out as students read the chapter. [BASIC]

❏ **Enrichment Activity, CRF** Students design a simulation of slowed reaction time. [ADVANCED]

Lesson Plan

Lesson: Pressure to Drink

Pacing

20 minutes

Objectives

1. Identify three pressures that tempt teens to drink alcohol.

Standards Covered

1.1 Explain the relationship between positive health behaviors and the prevention of injury, illness, disease and premature death.

1.4 Analyze how the family, peers, and community influence the health of individuals.

3.4 Develop strategies to improve or maintain personal, family, and community health.

4.2 Analyze how messages from media and other sources influence health behaviors.

4.4 Analyze how information from peers influences health.

KEY

SE = Student Edition   **ATE** = Annotated Teacher Edition

CRF = Chapter Resource File

FOCUS

❏ **Bellringer, ATE** Students complete the following statement: "When I am a parent, I will tell my child ______________________ about alcohol."

❏ **Bellringer Transparency** Use this transparency as students enter the classroom and find their seats.

❏ **Start Off Write, SE** Ask students to write an answer to the following question: "How might you feel pressured to drink?"

MOTIVATE

❏ **Discussion, Responding to Peer Pressure, ATE** Students consider the best responses to make when faced with pressure from peers to drink alcohol. [GENERAL]

Lesson Plan *continued*

TEACH

❏ **Life Skill Builder, Refusal Skills, ATE** Students respond to and role-play refusal situations. [GENERAL]

❏ **Refusal Skills, CRF** Students complete a worksheet on refusal skills. [GENERAL]

CLOSE

❏ **Lesson Quiz, ATE** Students answer 5 questions about pressure to drink.

❏ **Lesson Quiz, CRF** Students answer 6 questions about pressure to drink.

❏ **Concept Review, CRF** This exercise reinforces the material covered in the lesson.

HOMEWORK

❏ **Lesson Review, SE** Assign questions 1–4 for review, homework, or quiz.

OTHER RESOURCE OPTIONS

❏ **go.hrw.com** For worksheets, videos, and other teaching aids related to this chapter, visit the HRW Web site and type in the keyword HD4AL8.

❏ **VideoSelect** Videos related to the chapter topics may be found at go.hrw.com. Type in the keyword HD4AL8V.

❏ **Guided Audio CD Program Alcohol** The audio program is a reading of the chapter content for ELL students, auditory learners, and struggling readers.

❏ **Directed Reading, CRF** This worksheet is to be filled out as students read the chapter. [BASIC]

❏ **Enrichment Activity, CRF** Students report on a biography of someone who overcame internal and external pressures to make bad choices. [ADVANCED]

Lesson Plan

Lesson: Deciding Not to Drink

Pacing

25 minutes

Objectives

1. Identify three steps you would make when deciding not to drink alcohol.

2. Identify two ways to resist internal pressures to drink.

Standards Covered

1.1 Explain the relationship between positive health behaviors and the prevention of injury, illness, disease and other health problems.

1.4 Describe how family and peers influence the health of adolescents.

3.4 Demonstrate strategies to improve or maintain personal and family health.

4.2 Analyze how messages from media and other sources influence health behaviors.

4.4 Analyze how information from peers influences health.

KEY
SE = Student Edition **ATE** = Annotated Teacher Edition
CRF = Chapter Resource File

FOCUS

❏ **Bellringer, ATE** Students list their own top five reasons for not drinking alcohol.

❏ **Bellringer Transparency** Use this transparency as students enter the classroom and find their seats.

❏ **Start Off Write, SE** Ask students to write an answer to the following question: "What should you ask yourself when deciding not to drink?"

MOTIVATE

❏ **Group Activity, Short Play, ATE** Student groups write and perform a short play depicting a teen faced with the decision not to drink. **[GENERAL]**

TEACH

❏ **Debate, Drinking Under Adult Supervision ATE** Pose this question to students: "Should teens be allowed to drink alcohol if supervised by an adult?" **[GENERAL]**

❏ **Concept Mapping, CRF** Students create a concept map about internal pressures. **[GENERAL]**

Lesson Plan *continued*

CLOSE

❏ **Lesson Quiz, ATE** Students answer 2 questions about deciding not to drink.

❏ **Lesson Quiz, CRF** Students answer 6 questions about deciding not to drink.

❏ **Concept Review, CRF** This exercise reinforces the material covered in the lesson.

HOMEWORK

❏ **Lesson Review, SE** Assign questions 1–3 for review, homework, or quiz.

❏ **Decision-Making Skills, CRF** Students prepare a pocket-sized booklet of decision-making skills. [GENERAL]

OTHER RESOURCE OPTIONS

❏ **Internet Connect** Drugs and Alcohol Abuse, HealthLinks Code HD4029. Students research Internet sources about alcohol.

❏ **go.hrw.com** For worksheets, videos, and other teaching aids related to this chapter, visit the HRW Web site and type in the keyword HD4AL8.

❏ **VideoSelect** Videos related to the chapter topics may be found at go.hrw.com. Type in the keyword HD4AL8V.

❏ **Guided Audio CD Program Alcohol** The audio program is a reading of the chapter content for ELL students, auditory learners, and struggling readers.

❏ **Directed Reading, CRF** This worksheet is to be filled out as students read the chapter. [BASIC]

❏ **Enrichment Activity, CRF** Students analyze the pressures they feel and how they can deal with them. [ADVANCED]

Lesson Plan

Lesson: Alcoholism

Pacing

45 minutes

Objectives

1. Compare physical dependence and psychological dependence.

2. Describe how alcoholism can affect a person's social, mental, and emotional health.

3. Identify three factors that contribute to alcoholism.

4. Describe how a person can overcome alcoholism.

Standards Covered

1.1 Explain the relationship between positive health behaviors and the prevention of injury, illness, disease and other health problems.

1.4 Describe how family and peers influence the health of adolescents.

3.4 Demonstrate strategies to improve or maintain personal and family health.

6.2 Analyze how health-related decisions are influenced by individuals, family, and community values

6.3 Predict how decisions regarding health behaviors have consequences for self and others.

> **KEY**
> **SE** = Student Edition   **ATE** = Annotated Teacher Edition
> **CRF** = Chapter Resource File

FOCUS

❏ **Bellringer, ATE** Students make a list of criteria that they think could be used to diagnose alcoholism.

❏ **Bellringer Transparency** Use this transparency as students enter the classroom and find their seats.

❏ **Start Off Write, SE** Ask students to write an answer to the following question: "What causes alcoholism?"

MOTIVATE

❏ **Discussion, Who Can Have Alcoholism? ATE** Students consider what type of person they think could become addicted to alcohol. [GENERAL]

Lesson Plan *continued*

TEACH

❑ **Teaching Transparency, Warning Signs of Teen Alcohol Abuse** Use this graphic to help students recognize the warning signs.

❑ **Life Skill Builder, Making Good Decisions, ATE** Students consider the consequences and alternatives of going to parents about an older brother who is drinking 6 beers a day. [GENERAL]

❑ **Demonstration, Guest Speaker, ATE** A counselor who works directly with teens addicted to alcohol discusses how to deal with peers who may have problems with alcohol [GENERAL]

❑ **Cross-Disciplinary: Language Arts, CRF** Students write a letter to someone (real or imaginary) who is suffering from alcoholism telling the person how the illness makes the student feel. [GENERAL]

CLOSE

❑ **Lesson Quiz, ATE** Students answer 3 questions about alcoholism.

❑ **Lesson Quiz, CRF** Students answer 6 questions about deciding not to drink.

❑ **Concept Review, CRF** This exercise reinforces the material covered in the lesson.

HOMEWORK

❑ **Lesson Review, SE** Assign questions 1–5 for review, homework, or quiz.

OTHER RESOURCE OPTIONS

❑ **Internet Connect** Alcoholism, HealthLinks Code HD4007. Students research Internet sources about alcoholism.

❑ **go.hrw.com** For worksheets, videos, and other teaching aids related to this chapter, visit the HRW Web site and type in the keyword HD4AL8.

❑ **VideoSelect** Videos related to the chapter topics may be found at go.hrw.com. Type in the keyword HD4AL8V.

❑ **Guided Audio CD Program Alcohol** The audio program is a reading of the chapter content for ELL students, auditory learners, and struggling readers.

❑ **Directed Reading, CRF** This worksheet is to be filled out as students read the chapter. [BASIC]

❑ **Enrichment Activity, CRF** Students draw a picture, sketch, or diagram showing how a person who has alcoholism differs from a casual user of alcohol. [ADVANCED]

Lesson Plan

End of Chapter Review and Assessment

Pacing

90 minutes

> **KEY**
> **SE** = Student Edition   **ATE** = Annotated Teacher Edition
> **CRF** = Chapter Resource File

REVIEW

❑ **Chapter Review, SE** Assign questions to review the material for this chapter. Use the assignment guide to customize review for lessons covered.

❑ **Concept Review, CRF** Vocabulary and concept review for each lesson. [GENERAL]

ASSESSMENT

❑ **Chapter Test, Alcohol, CRF** Assign questions for general level chapter assessment. [GENERAL]

ALTERNATIVE ASSESSMENT

❑ **Alternative Assessment, Warning Label, ATE** Assign this activity for general level chapter assessment. [GENERAL]

❑ **Alternative Assessment, Editorial, ATE** Assign this activity for general level chapter assessment. [GENERAL]

❑ **Alternative Assessment, City Hall Speech, ATE** Assign this activity for general level chapter assessment. [GENERAL]

❑ **Alternative Assessment, Letter, ATE** Assign this activity for general level chapter assessment. [GENERAL]

❑ **Performance-Based Assessment, How Alcohol Affects You, CRF** Students create and act out skits that demonstrate knowledge of alcohol and its effects. [GENERAL]

❑ **Test Generator One-Stop Planner** Create a customized homework, quiz, or test using the HRW Test Generator program.

❑ **Test Item Listing, CRF** Use the Test Item Listing to identify questions to use in a customized homework, quiz, or test.

Parent Letter

Alcohol

Dear Parent/Guardian:

During the next few weeks, your child will learn about the risks associated with alcohol consumption. Your child will learn about how alcohol affects the body, the ability to make decisions, the family, and society. He or she will gain information on why driving under the influence of alcohol is so dangerous.

Your child will also practice refusal skills and decision-making skills so that he or she can make good choices and stick to them. The course will cover positive peer pressure and how friends and family can help one another to make healthy choices they can be proud of.

Your child will be sharing information about alcohol with you in the At-Home Activity. You could also write a letter to your child praising the good qualities you see in him or her and telling him or her the things you hope for his or her future. Tell your child any concerns you have about alcohol use. Your signature on the worksheet will indicate that your child has completed his or her portion of the At-Home Activity.

Thank you in advance for your time, cooperation, and support.

Sincerely,

____

Health Teacher

Carta a los Padres/al Tutor

El alcohol

Estimado(s) Padres/Tutor:

Durante las próximas semanas, su hijo/a va a aprender de los riesgos del consumo del alcohol. Aprenderá de los efectos del alcohol en el cuerpo, en la capacidad de hacer decisiones, en la familia y en toda la sociedad. El/ella estudiará información sobre los peligros de manejar bajo la influencia del alcohol.

Su hijo/a va a practicar las acciones de decir "no" y de hacer buenas decisiones para que pueda salir airoso/a de situaciones difíciles con los valores intactos. La clase de Salud tratará con la influencia positiva de los socios y cómo los amigos y familiares pueden ayudarse a hacer decisiones valiosas.

Su hijo/a va a compartir con Ud. información sobre el alcohol durante la Actividad En Casa. También sería una acción impactante escribirle una carta personal elogiando los buenos puntos de su carácter y relatando sus esperanzas para él o ella en el futuro. Comparta sus inquietudes o dudas sobre el uso del alcohol. Su firma en la hoja de trabajo verificará que su hijo/a le haya entregado la carta y que Uds. juntos la hayan discutido.

Gracias anticipadas por su tiempo, cooperación y apoyo.

Atentamente,

____

Maestro/a de Salud

Performance-Based Assessment

Teacher's Notes

INTRODUCTION

This performance-based assessment consists of students responding to real life scenarios in which their knowledge about alcohol and its effects could be useful.

TIME REQUIRED One 45 minute class period

Students will need 35–40 minutes to complete their responses to the scenarios and 5 minutes to answer the analysis questions.

PBA RATINGS   Easy ←——1——2——3——4——→ Hard
   Teacher Prep—3
   Student Set-Up—1
   Concept Level—1
   Clean Up—1

ADVANCE PREPARATION

Using the following sample situations as a guide, prepare enough situations for each group to have one or two.

- Someone asks you, "Why do people get so goofy when they drink alcohol?"

- Someone says to you, "This newspaper article says this guy's blood alcohol concentration was 0.08. What's a blood alcohol concentration?"

- Someone at a family gathering is getting a little intoxicated. This person drove to the party. What could you do to protect the person and the other people on the road? Who in the group can help you?

- Your brother says, "Jenny's uncle has cirrhosis. What's that?" Explain.

- You're invited to go boating. You see the supplies waiting to be loaded for the trip. There are three six-packs of beer. What would be a safe decision?

- Someone says, "You're feeling down today? I've heard alcohol can make you feel better. What do you think?"

PERFORMANCE

At the end of the test students should turn in the following items:
   - their notes on other class members' performances
   - an answer to the analysis question

EVALUATION

The following is a recommended breakdown for evaluating student performance:
   30% Appropriate class behavior
   25% Group response to situations
   35% Notes kept by student
   10% Analysis question on worksheet

Answer Key

Directed Reading

LESSON: ALCOHOL AND YOUR BODY

1. fermentation of plants
2. beverage alcohol in moderate amounts will not kill you; the other alcohols can kill you even if you have just a little bit
3. the brain and the spinal cord
4. your thinking, memory, and judgment are impaired
5. 10,000
6. alcohol

LESSON: IMMEDIATE EFFECTS OF ALCOHOL

7. b
8. the physical and mental changes produced by drinking alcohol.
9. thinking clearly
10. consequences
11. mood

LESSON: LONG-TERM EFFECTS OF ALCOHOL

12. cirrhosis
13. brain
14. tolerance
15. Self-control and abstinence are less likely and it's harder to recognize danger.
16. fetal alcohol syndrome

LESSON: ALCOHOL AND DECISION-MAKING

17. b
18. c

LESSON: ALCOHOL, DRIVING, AND INJURIES

19. drinking
20. reaction time
21. Drivers who have been drinking alcohol cannot think clearly or steer or brake properly because their reaction time is slowed.

LESSON: PRESSURE TO DRINK

22. deaths
23. I
24. I
25. N
26. I
27. Answers may vary. Sample answer: drinking is attractive and normal
28. Answers may vary. Sample answer: you can feel that everyone drinks to have a good time.

LESSON: DECIDING NOT TO DRINK

29. values
30. consequence
31. Answers may vary. Sample answers: talk to someone; take time to think about what you really need

LESSON: ALCOHOLISM

32. a disease where a person is physically and emotionally addicted to alcohol.
33. b
34. d
35. drug
36. genes
37. recovery

Concept Mapping

LESSON: ALCOHOL AND YOUR BODY

When you swallow *alcohol* it is absorbed by your stomach and *small intestine* and quickly enters the *bloodstream*; it is carried by your *blood* to your *central nervous system* where it affects your *brain*.

LESSON: DECIDING NOT TO DRINK

Answers may vary. Sample answer: When choosing whether to *drink alcohol* or *refuse alcohol*, consider your *options, consequences*, and *values*, including *negative effects*, such as *feeling guilty*.

Concept Review

LESSON: ALCOHOL AND YOUR BODY

1. Alcohol travels throughout the body and affects the central nervous system (the brain and the spinal cord), controlling speech, thinking, memory, etc.).
2. The percentage amount of alcohol in the bloodstream
3. women's bodies absorb and metabolize alcohol differently than men, a person's general health, amount of sleep a person has had, medications a person is taking, and a person's expectations

LESSON: IMMEDIATE EFFECTS OF ALCOHOL

4. A
5. A
6. N
7. A
8. N
9. A
10. A
11. N
12. Alcohol decreases your ability to recognize or protect yourself from danger, makes you lose concentration and coordination so you can be injured more easily, and increases mood swings, which can cause fights.

LESSON: LONG-TERM EFFECTS OF ALCOHOL

13. d
14. when your body needs more alcohol to get the same effect
15. Her inhibitions are lowered and her ability to recognize danger or take precautions are impaired.
16. a group of birth defects that can affect a fetus if the mother drinks during pregnancy

LESSON: ALCOHOL AND DECISION-MAKING

17. a
18. c

LESSON: ALCOHOL, DRIVING, AND INJURIES

19. Alcohol slows down the time from when you see a problem to when you can react, or do something about it. This is very dangerous when driving a vehicle.
20. drunk driving

LESSON: PRESSURE TO DRINK

21. I
22. E
23. E
24. I
25. E
26. I
27. I
28. E

LESSON: DECIDING NOT TO DRINK

29. d
30. a
31. b
32. Answers may vary. Sample answers: talk to someone; think through your feelings and identify the problems; write down your thoughts

LESSON: ALCOHOLISM

33. PH
34. PS
35. PH (could be PS too)
36. PS
37. trying alcohol; feelings that seem too strong to handle; genetic factors; family history
38. the decision to stop drinking
39. doctors; counselors; groups like Alcoholics Anonymous.

Refusal Skills

LESSON: PRESSURE TO DRINK

1. Sample answer: "No, thanks."
2. Sample answer: "I'm a soda fan, myself. Do you want some?"
3. Sample answer: "Not for me."
4. Sample answer: Carefully remove his/her arm from your sleeve and go find someone else to talk to.
5. Sample answer: Find another friend in the crowd you can stay with.

6. Sample answer: Look around the crowd for people who could support you.

LESSON: PRESSURE TO DRINK

Accept all reasonable responses. The game board design should have at least 10 squares, rules, a way to move around the board, and opportunities to make decisions about alcohol and to practice avoiding and refusing alcohol.

Decision-Making Skills

LESSON: DECIDING NOT TO DRINK

1. Answers may vary. Accept all reasonable answers for this worksheet.
2. Answers may vary. Accept all reasonable answers for this worksheet.
3. Answers may vary. Accept all reasonable answers for this worksheet.
4. Answers may vary. Accept all reasonable answers for this worksheet.
5. Answers may vary. Accept all reasonable answers for this worksheet.
6. Answers may vary. Accept all reasonable answers for this worksheet.

LESSON: ALCOHOL AND DECISION-MAKING

The booklet should have the steps of making a good decision, some refusal skills, and other information to personalize it for the student.

Cross-Disciplinary: Science

LESSON: ALCOHOL AND YOUR BODY

The student should have a chart or paragraph comparing how alcohol is used by the body with how healthful foods and drinks are used by the body.

Cross-Disciplinary: Language Arts

LESSON: ALCOHOLISM

The student will have either a letter or a poem. Look for specific, believable details that show that the student has some understanding of alcoholism.

Quiz

LESSON: ALCOHOL AND YOUR BODY
1. c
2. c
3. d
4. c
5. a
6. b

LESSON: IMMEDIATE EFFECTS OF ALCOHOL
1. d
2. a
3. c
4. b
5. a
6. c

LESSON: LONG-TERM EFFECTS OF ALCOHOL
1. a
2. c
3. c
4. b
5. c
6. a

LESSON: ALCOHOL AND DECISION-MAKING
1. b
2. d
3. c
4. b
5. a
6. c

LESSON: ALCOHOL, DRIVING, AND INJURIES
1. d
2. c
3. c
4. c
5. a
6. b

LESSON: PRESSURE TO DRINK
1. b
2. a
3. a
4. c
5. a
6. b

LESSON: DECIDING NOT TO DRINK

1. b
2. d
3. c
4. c
5. a
6. b

LESSON: ALCOHOLISM

1. d
2. a
3. c
4. c
5. a
6. b

Chapter Test

1. psychological
2. blood alcohol concentration
3. tolerance
4. recovery
5. d
6. b
7. b
8. c
9. d
10. d
11. d
12. b
13. b
14. d
15. a drug that slows body functioning
16. the physical and mental changes produced by drinking alcohol
17. Fetal alcohol syndrome is a group of birth defects that affect a fetus that has been exposed to alcohol.
18. Physical effects caused by alcohol use include headache, nausea, and stomach upset. Someone gets a hangover after drinking.
19. Answers may vary. Sample answer: reaction time is slowed; inhibitions are down; it's harder to see risks; coordination is poor; and judgement is impaired
20. Answers may vary. Sample answer: Alcohol impairs a person's ability to think, which affects his or her ability to analyze situations and make good decisions. So, someone who has been drinking alcohol is more likely to choose to engage in unsafe or unhealthy activities.
21. Sample answer: Drinking *alcohol* can lead to *alcoholism*, which can cause *cirrhosis* unless a person begins *recovery*, and *dependence*, which can be *physical* or *psychological*.

Performance-Based Assessment

Answers may vary. Accept all reasonable answers.

Datasheet for In-Text Activity

Answers may vary. Accept all reasonable answers.

Life Skills: Evaluating Media Messages

LESSON: IMMEDIATE EFFECT OF ALCOHOL

Answers may vary. Accept all reasonable answers.

Life Skills: Coping

LESSON: LONG-TERM EFFECTS OF ALCOHOL

1. Answers may vary. Sample answer: A person with cirrhosis of the liver would be severely limited in what they could do and enjoy physically. They could also suffer from brain damage as a result and might require assistance in many everyday activities.

2. Answers may vary. Sample answer: People around this person would have to be available to give constant care and provide assistance around the clock.

3. I could help care for this person by providing support and companionship and by doing household chores and running errands.

Enrichment Activity

LESSON: ALCOHOL AND YOUR BODY

Answers may vary. An acceptable assignment will include a summary of a historical or literary event involving alcohol and an analysis of what effect (if any) alcohol had on the outcome of the event and what might have been different if alcohol had not been involved.

LESSON: IMMEDIATE EFFECTS OF ALCOHOL

Answers may vary. An acceptable assignment will include an opinion about whether or not people should be responsible for their actions shown under the influence of a drug or alcohol. Students should back up their opinion with reasons.

LESSON: LONG-TERM EFFECTS OF ALCOHOL

Answers may vary. An acceptable assignment will include the phrases the student brainstormed and an indication of which three he or she thought were best.

LESSON: ALCOHOL AND DECISION-MAKING

Answers may vary. An acceptable assignment will be a paragraph giving the student's views about the best way to teach people about alcohol so they can make informed decisions.

LESSON: ALCOHOL, DRIVING, AND INJURIES

Answers may vary. An acceptable assignment will include a plan for a simulation of slowed reaction time that is safe and uses only materials that are commonly found at home or at school. All projects should be cleared through the teacher before being carried out.

LESSON: PRESSURE TO DRINK

Answers may vary. An acceptable assignment will include a biography sheet listing the name, birth date, birthplace, and a summary of the life of the person studied. It should be clear how this person resisted internal and external pressures to make bad choices.

LESSON: DECIDING NOT TO DRINK

Answers may vary. An acceptable assignment will list internal and external pressures and what might help you deal with them. Accept parent signatures in lieu of the assignment if the student chooses that option.

LESSON: ALCOHOLISM

Answers may vary. An acceptable assignment will be a three-dimensional model which shows differences between how a casual drinker reacts to alcohol and the way an alcoholic reacts to alcohol.

Health Inventory

Answers may vary. Accept all reasonable answers.

Health Behavior Contract

Answers may vary. Accept all reasonable answers.

At-Home Activity

The parent signature is proof that the assignment is satisfactory.

Selected Spanish Answers

CONCEPT REVIEW

33. DF
34. DP
35. DF (could be DP too)
36. DP

Alcohol

MULTIPLE CHOICE

1. Alcohol affects the part of your brain that controls
   a. hair and eye color.
   b. circulation.
   c. breathing.
   d. behavior.
   Answer: D   Difficulty: 1   Section: 1   Objective: 1

2. As the body processes alcohol the blood becomes more acidic, causing the uncomfortable headache and nausea called
   a. a depressant.
   b. a hangover.
   c. blood alcohol concentration.
   d. an inhibition.
   Answer: B   Difficulty: 1   Section: 2   Objective: 1

3. When a person cannot limit his drinking to appropriate times or moderate amounts it is called
   a. depression.
   b. coma.
   c. alcohol abuse.
   d. cirrhosis.
   Answer: C   Difficulty: 1   Section: 3   Objective: 1

4. When someone has been drinking he or she is more likely to
   a. be cautious.
   b. see danger everywhere.
   c. take physical risks.
   d. All of the above
   Answer: C   Difficulty: 1   Section: 4   Objective: 1

5. Even one drink can slow a driver's
   a. impulse control.
   b. heart rate.
   c. reaction time.
   d. blood alcohol concentration.
   Answer: C   Difficulty: 1   Section: 5   Objective: 1

6. Seeing adults drink and advertisements for beer and other alcohol can make teenagers
   a. feel curious about alcohol.
   b. see drinking as desirable and mature.
   c. think that alcohol makes you happy.
   d. All of the above
   Answer: D   Difficulty: 1   Section: 6   Objective: 2

7. Alcoholism is a chronic disease, so it is not curable
   a. and there's no treatment.
   b. but it is treatable.
   c. but it can be solved with medication.
   d. because it is genetic.
   Answer: B   Difficulty: 1   Section: 8   Objective: 4

8. What part of the body does alcohol mainly affect?
   a. digestive system
   b. respiratory system
   c. central nervous system
   d. circulatory system
   Answer: C   Difficulty: 1   Section: 1   Objective: 1

9. Why does the amount of alcohol concentrated in your blood increase so rapidly if you drink more than one drink an hour?
   a. Your blood slows down.
   b. The liver has shut down.
   c. The liver can't process it fast enough.
   d. You don't have food in your stomach.
   Answer: C   Difficulty: 1   Section: 1   Objective: 2

10. How a person reacts to alcohol is affected by his or her health, his or her sex, the amount of sleep he or she has gotten and
    a. skin tone.
    b. the time of day.
    c. the type of drinking container used.
    d. any medications the person is taking.
    Answer: D   Difficulty: 1   Section: 1   Objective: 3

11. As you drink you become mildly intoxicated and may feel lightheaded; as intoxication increases it becomes difficult to
    a. drink more.
    b. feel emotions.
    c. get violent.
    d. do anything requiring coordination.

    Answer: D   Difficulty: 1   Section: 2   Objective: 3

12. What are some of the risks you take if you decide to drink one evening?
    a. mood swings and loss of coordination
    b. loss of skin and hair tissue
    c. cancer and tumors
    d. respiratory disease

    Answer: A   Difficulty: 1   Section: 2   Objective: 2

13. If you drink way too much alcohol at one time what do you risk?
    a. being silly
    b. having people laugh at you
    c. poisoning and death
    d. walking crooked

    Answer: C   Difficulty: 1   Section: 2   Objective: 2

14. Drinking before your brain is fully mature may cause what to happen?
    a. Your brain becomes impaired.
    b. You lose your hair.
    c. You get cancer.
    d. Your skin becomes wrinkled.

    Answer: A   Difficulty: 1   Section: 3   Objective: 1

15. What part of your body does alcohol-related cirrhosis affect?
    a. brain
    b. central nervous system
    c. liver
    d. blood

    Answer: C   Difficulty: 1   Section: 3   Objective: 1

16. Why are pregnant women warned not to drink alcohol?
    a. It can cause weight gain.
    b. It can lead to divorce.
    c. It can cause fetal alcohol syndrome.
    d. It can lead to extra-long pregnancies.

    Answer: C   Difficulty: 1   Section: 3   Objective: 2

17. What is a word for the mental or psychological processes that restrain your actions, emotions, and thoughts?
    a. restrainers
    b. inhibitions
    c. demotions
    d. consequences

    Answer: B   Difficulty: 1   Section: 4   Objective: 1

18. When you've drunk some alcohol it's harder to
    a. act funny.
    b. party.
    c. be with people.
    d. recognize risks.

    Answer: D   Difficulty: 1   Section: 4   Objective: 1

19. Fights, crimes, abuse, vandalism and robbery are more likely if what is involved?
    a. cars
    b. property
    c. alcohol
    d. depression

    Answer: C   Difficulty: 1   Section: 4   Objective: 2

20. When a person drinks one drink his or her ability to drive an automobile is
    a. unchanged.
    b. better than ever.
    c. terrible.
    d. somewhat affected.

    Answer: D   Difficulty: 1   Section: 5   Objective: 1

21. The only sure way to avoid alcohol-related injuries and death is to ride with someone only if
    a. he or she can walk straight.
    b. you are in the front seat.
    c. he or she has not been drinking
    d. he or she has less than three drinks.

    Answer: C   Difficulty: 1   Section: 5   Objective: 1

22. Groups like SADD and MADD and a combination of stronger laws and stricter enforcement have reduced
    a. the number of people who drink.
    b. the amount of alcohol sold.
    c. the number of alcohol-related car accidents.
    d. the number of alcohol-related suicides.

    Answer: C   Difficulty: 1   Section: 5   Objective: 2

23. Most teens have an inner need to be part of a
    a. team.   c. school.
    b. group.   d. class.

    Answer: B   Difficulty: 1   Section: 6   Objective: 1

24. Low self-esteem, trying to escape unpleasant feelings, and wanting to impress others are all reasons teens may
    a. drink.   c. be careful.
    b. drive.   d. give up.

    Answer: A   Difficulty: 1   Section: 6   Objective: 1

25. Seeing people drinking at parties, sporting events, and restaurants can make you think that
    a. everyone drinks.   c. everyone is grown up.
    b. everyone drinks too much.   d. everyone is looking at you.

    Answer: A   Difficulty: 1   Section: 6   Objective: 1

26. When you are trying to make a big decision you should
    a. follow someone's example.   c. drink some alcohol to help you think.
    b. think about what your values are.   d. respond to the pressures you feel.

    Answer: B   Difficulty: 1   Section: 7   Objective: 1

27. If you're feeling lonely or bad about yourself you should
    a. shake it off.   c. get some new friends.
    b. hang out with friends.   d. talk to an adult you trust.

    Answer: D   Difficulty: 1   Section: 7   Objective: 2

28. When you're feeling a lot of pressure you should
    a. find something to do.   c. take some time to think.
    b. take something to relax you. d. go have a good time.

    Answer: C   Difficulty: 1   Section: 7   Objective: 2

29. Physical dependence has to do with the body while psychological dependence has to do with
    a. the people around you.   c. a need for a psychiatrist.
    b. the values and beliefs that you have.   d. emotions and thoughts.

    Answer: D   Difficulty: 2   Section: 8   Objective: 1

30. When someone's friendships, work, daily routine and the way he or she spends money all revolve around alcohol it is likely he or she
    a. has alcoholism.   c. is already too damaged to quit.
    b. can easily stop drinking.   d. has self-esteem.

    Answer: A   Difficulty: 1   Section: 8   Objective: 2

31. The first step to overcoming alcoholism is deciding to
    a. drink less.   c. stop drinking.
    b. drink only at night.   d. quit work.

    Answer: C   Difficulty: 1   Section: 8   Objective: 4

32. What effect does alcohol have on a person's ability to make decisions?
    a. makes it easier to think
    b. calms the emotions
    c. increases inhibitions
    d. makes it harder to see risks
    Answer: D   Difficulty: 1   Section: 4   Objective: 1

33. When alcohol gets to the brain, it impairs judgment, coordination, and
    a. lung capacity.
    b. vision.
    c. nerve development.
    d. All of the above
    Answer: B   Difficulty: 1   Section: 5   Objective: 1

34. Which of the following is an internal pressure that might make someone more likely to try alcohol?
    a. cirrhosis
    b. low self-esteem
    c. refusal skills
    d. confidence
    Answer: B   Difficulty: 1   Section: 6   Objective: 1

35. The brain and spinal cord are part of what system?
    a. circulatory
    b. digestive
    c. nervous
    d. brain
    Answer: C   Difficulty: 1   Section: 1   Objective: 1

36. What is the only thing that can get your BAC down?
    a. coffee
    b. a shower
    c. food
    d. time
    Answer: D   Difficulty: 1   Section: 1   Objective: 3

37. Alcohol poisoning
    a. is a drug overdose.
    b. is caused by drinking too much alcohol.
    c. can be fatal.
    d. All of the above
    Answer: D   Difficulty: 1   Section: 1   Objective: 1

38. Alcohol reaches the brain
    a. through the small intestine.
    b. in 10–15 heartbeats.
    c. through the heart.
    d. All of the above
    Answer: D   Difficulty: 1   Section: 1   Objective: 1

39. The best way to avoid inuries and death from drunk driving is to
    a. wear your seat belt.
    b. never ride with someone who has been drinking.
    c. take public transportation.
    d. None of the above
    Answer: B   Difficulty: 1   Section: 5   Objective: 2

40. The body's chemical need for a drug is called
    a. tolerance.
    b. physical dependence.
    c. alcoholism.
    d. None of the above
    Answer: B   Difficulty: 1   Section: 8   Objective: 1

41. Which of the following is a factor that might influence whether a person develops alcoholism?
    a. height
    b. reaction time
    c. knowledge about alcohol
    d. genes
    Answer: D   Difficulty: 1   Section: 8   Objective: 3

COMPLETION

42. Some people think that ___________________ makes their feelings seem more bearable.
    Answer: alcohol   Difficulty: 1   Section: 8   Objective: 3

43. Many teens feel that by drinking they will be more accepted by their
    ___________________.
    Answer: peers   Difficulty: 1   Section: 6   Objective: 1

44. Drinking alcohol before or while operating machinery or playing sports makes
    ___________________ more likely.
    Answer: injuries   Difficulty: 1   Section: 5   Objective: 3

45. When people loosen up control of their emotions while drinking, social situations may
    become more ___________________.
    Answer: violent   Difficulty: 1   Section: 4   Objective: 4

46. Regular, heavy drinking can lead to alcohol ___________________ so people find they
    have to drink more for the same effect.
    Answer: tolerance   Difficulty: 1   Section: 3   Objective: 1

47. As ___________________ increases, your feelings and behavior become exaggerated and
    your judgment and self-control decrease.
    Answer: intoxication   Difficulty: 1   Section: 2   Objective: 1

48. A BAC or BAL of 0.08 percent means a person has eight parts alcohol per 10,000 parts of
    ___________________.
    Answer: blood   Difficulty: 1   Section: 1   Objective: 2

49. Curiosity is an ___________________ pressure.
    Answer: internal   Difficulty: 1   Section: 6   Objective: 1

50. Parents who drink wine only with meals provide ___________________ pressure.
    Answer: internal and external
                            Difficulty: 1   Section: 6   Objective: 1

51. Friends telling you "everybody's doing it "provides ___________________ pressure.
    Answer: external   Difficulty: 1   Section: 6   Objective: 1

52. Addiction is an ___________________ pressure. (internal or external)
    Answer: internal   Difficulty: 1   Section: 5   Objective: 1

53. A magazine advertisement provides ___________________ pressure.
    Answer: external   Difficulty: 1   Section: 6   Objective: 1

54. Whenever Sam has had a rough day he unwinds with a couple of beers. It's hard for him
    now to feel relaxed without them because he has developed a ___________________
    dependence on alcohol.
    Answer: psychological
                            Difficulty: 1   Section: 8   Objective: 1

55. When a policeman stops someone he thinks might have been drinking, one test he can
    use is the ___________________ test to see how much alcohol is in the blood.
    Answer: BAL   Difficulty: 1   Section: 1   Objective: 2

56. Some people drink alcohol to relax, but after a while they find that they require more
    alcohol to relax because they have built up a ___________________.
    Answer: tolerance   Difficulty: 1   Section: 3   Objective: 1

57. Maria's uncle goes to Alcoholics Anonymous at least once a week as part of his
_____________________ from alcohol.

Answer: recovery   Difficulty: 1   Section: 8   Objective: 4

SHORT ANSWER

58. Name two factors that make one person's reaction to alcohol different than someone else's.

Sample answer:
Different sexes and body builds absorb alcohol at different rates; general health, amount of sleep, and medication can all affect reaction.

Difficulty: 2   Section: 1   Objective: 3

59. Why does alcohol make you less aware of other people's feelings?

Sample answer:
Alcohol interferes with your ability to think and make judgments.

Difficulty: 1   Section: 2   Objective: 2

60. Name two activities besides driving that can be dangerous for people affected by alcohol.

Sample answer: operating machinery, playing sports, water activities

Difficulty: 2   Section: 5   Objective: 3

61. What are two things that a person wanting to overcome alcoholism should do?

Answer:
Answers may vary. Sample answers: decide to stop drinking, seek medical help and counseling, join a group like AA

Difficulty: 2   Section: 8   Objective: 4

62. How does alcohol enter the bloodstream?

Sample answer: It is absorbed through the walls of the stomach and small intestine.

Difficulty: 1   Section:1   Objective: 1

63 How would you be affected by alcohol if you had a BAC of 0.08?

Sample answer: There would be definite impairment of motor skills and reaction times.

Difficulty: 2   Section: 7   Objective: 2

64. Name one long-term effect of drinking?

Sample answer: cirrhosis, alcohol abuse, tolerance, brain impairment

Difficulty: 2   Section: 3   Objective: 1

65. What is reaction time and how does alcohol affect it?

Sample answer:
It is the time from when you first have a stimulus (see something, hear something, etc.) to the time you react. Alcohol slows reaction time.

Difficulty: 2   Section: 5   Objective: 1

66. Why do you think alcohol can cause so much damage to the liver?

Sample answer:
The liver is the primary organ in the body that removes alcohol from the body, so it has the most contact with the damaging effects of alcohol.

Difficulty: 2   Section: 3   Objective: 1

67. Other than fetal alcohol syndrome, why might it be harmful for a woman to drink while she is pregnant?

    Sample answer:

    The effects of alcohol, such as loss of judgment, loss of coordination, and reduced inhibitions might lead a pregnant woman to take risks that could harm her or the fetus.

    Difficulty: 2   Section: 3   Objective: 2

68. Describe how somebody with a lack of inhibitions may act?

    Sample answer:

    They may talk with complete strangers, speak too loudly, take physical risks, misread other people's intentions and start fights, or cause injury to another person.

    Difficulty: 2   Section: 4   Objective: 1

69. What should you base your decision not to drink alcohol on?

    Sample answer: Your values

    Difficulty: 1   Section: 7   Objective: 1

70. Name two things you can do to resist an internal pressure to drink.

    Sample answer: improve your self-esteem and talk to a trusted adult

    Difficulty: 1   Section: 7   Objective: 2

71. List five warning signs of teen alcoholism.

    Sample answer:

    loss of interest in activities, uncharacteristic withdrawal from family and friends, heightened secrecy about actions and possessions, association with friends who drink, smell of alcohol or overuse of breath mints, association with an older crowd, association with known alcohol users, getting upset easily, frequent changes in emotions, defiance toward adults, skipping school, getting into trouble in school, change in appearance or hygiene

    Difficulty: 2   Section: 8   Objective: 2

72. List five reasons why people drink.

    Sample answer:

    depression, to fit into a group, because they feel powerless, because they don't like themselves, to get over the loss of a loved one

    Difficulty: 1   Section: 8   Objective: 3

73. Define recovery from alcoholism.

    Answer: Learning to live without alcohol.

    Difficulty: 1   Section: 8   Objective: 4

74. What is a depressant?

    Answer: A depressant is a drug that slows body fundtioning

    Difficulty: 1   Section: 1   Objective: 1

75. What is intoxication?

    Answer:

    Intoxication is the physical and mental changes produced by drinking alcohol

    Difficulty: 1   Section: 2   Objective: 1

76. What is fetal alcohol syndrome?

    Answer:

    Fetal alcohol syndrome is the group of birth defects that affect an unborn baby that has been exposed to alcohol.

    Difficulty: 1   Section: 2   Objective: 1

MATCHING

a. central nervous system
b. depressant
c. BAC
d. alcohol abuse
e. recovery
f. pregnancy
g. coma
h. internal pressure
i. relaxes
j. intoxication
k. alcohol poisoning
l. hangover
m. cirrhosis
n. tolerance
o. fetal alcohol syndrome
p. unclear thinking
q. inhibitions
r. consequences
s. stimulus
t. reaction time
u. concentration
v. internal
w. advertisements
x. external
y. values
z. alcoholism
aa. dependence

77. ____ the percentage of alcohol in the blood
Answer: C   Difficulty: 1   Section: 1   Objective: 1

78. ____ the brain and spinal cord
Answer: A   Difficulty: 1   Section: 3   Objective: 2

79. ____ the inability to drink moderately or at appropriate times
Answer: D   Difficulty: 1   Section: 3   Objective: 1

80. ____ drug that slows body functioning
Answer: B   Difficulty: 1   Section: 2   Objective: 1

81. ____ alcohol poisoning can cause this sleep-like condition that is very serious
Answer: G   Difficulty: 1   Section: 1   Objective: 1

82. ____ during this time a woman absolutely should not drink
Answer: F   Difficulty: 1   Section: 3   Objective: 2

83. ____ alcohol does this to your inhibitions
Answer: I   Difficulty: 1   Section: 4   Objective: 1

84. ____ the changes produced by drinking
Answer: J   Difficulty: 1   Section: 2   Objective: 1

85. ____ effect similar to a drug overdose
Answer: K   Difficulty: 1   Section: 2   Objective: 2

86. ____ disease that turns the liver to scar tissue
Answer: M   Difficulty: 1   Section: 3   Objective: 1

87. ____ uncomfortable physical effects from alcohol
Answer: L   Difficulty: 1   Section: 2   Objective: 1

88. ____ one of the effects of alcohol
Answer: P   Difficulty: 1   Section: 4   Objective: 1

89. ____ more alcohol needed for the same effect
Answer: N   Difficulty: 1   Section: 3   Objective: 2

90. ____ the time between a stimulus and a reaction
Answer: T   Difficulty: 1   Section: 5   Objective: 1

91. ____ group of birth defects caused by alcohol
Answer: O   Difficulty: 1   Section: 3   Objective: 2

92 ____ restraint of actions and emotions
Answer: Q   Difficulty: 1   Section: 4   Objective: 1

93. ____ possible results of your actions
Answer: R   Difficulty: 1   Section: 4   Objective: 2

94. ____ a sight, sound or thought causing a reaction
Answer: S   Difficulty: 1   Section: 5   Objective: 1

95. ____ one of the skills reduced by alcohol

    Answer: U   Difficulty: 1   Section: 5   Objective: 1, 2

96. ____ promotions designed to get you to buy a product

    Answer: W   Difficulty: 1   Section: 6   Objective: 1

97. ____ pressures from outside yourself

    Answer: X   Difficulty: 1   Section: 6   Objective: 1

98. ____ pressures from inside yourself

    Answer: V   Difficulty: 1   Section: 6   Objective: 1

99. ____ feelings and needs inside you

    Answer: H   Difficulty: 1   Section: 7   Objective: 1

100. ____ learning to live without alcohol

    Answer: E   Difficulty: 1   Section: 8   Objective: 4

101. ____ dependence on alcohol

    Answer: Z   Difficulty: 1   Section: 8   Objective: 1

102. ____ beliefs that are important to you

    Answer: Y   Difficulty: 1   Section: 7   Objective: 1

103. ____ physical, emotional or mental need

    Answer: AA   Difficulty: 1   Section: 8   Objective: 1

ESSAY

104. Explain what a hangover is and how someone gets a hangover.

    Sample answer:

    A hangover is an uncomfortable feeling after you drink alcohol (dizziness, headache, nausea). You get it because alcohol makes your blood more acidic.

    Difficulty: 2   Section: 2   Objective: 1

105. Why is a person more likely to be injured while he or she is drinking?

    Sample answer:

    The ability to think, judgment, coordination, vision, etc., are all impaired, so accidents can happen easily.

    Difficulty: 2   Section: 5   Objective: 3

106. Why does refusing to drink alcohol decrease your risk of getting injured or engaging in unhealthy behaviors?

    Sample answer:

    Alcohol impairs a person's ability to think, which affects his or her ability to analyze situations and make good decisions. Someone who has been drinking alcohol is more likely to choose to engage in unsafe or unhealthy activities.

    Difficulty: 2   Section: 6   Objective: 1

CONCEPT MAPPING

107. Use the following terms to create a concept map: *alcohol, alcoholism, recovery, dependence, physical, psychological,* and *cirrhosis.*

    Sample answer:

    Drinking *alcohol* can lead to *alcoholism*, which can cause *cirrhosis* unless a person begins *recovery*; and *dependence*, which can be *physical* or *psychological*.

    Difficulty: 3   Section: 8   Objective: 1–4

108. Use the following terms to complete the concept map below: *alcohol, small intestine, central nervous system, bloodstream, blood, stomach,* and *brain.*

When you swallow

it is absorbed by your   **it is carried by your**

and quickly enters the

to your

where it affects your

Sample answer:
> When you swallow *alcohol* it is absorbed by your *stomach* and *small intestine* and quickly enters the *bloodstream*; it is carried by your *blood* to you *central nervous system* where it affects your *brain.*

Difficulty: 3   Section: 1   Objective: 1